JOTD

Written, published and directed by

Hershel "Rabbs" Remer

a.k.a. the unixrabbi

Published by

Rabbs.com

Los Angeles, California

Foreword

by Rachel Goldstein, UNIX Administrator

Welcome to **JOTD** — the greatest geek adult humor book ever released on the market. Written by a professional comic/Solaris network administrator/rabbi, **JOTD** boldly makes fun of the world of computer technology, corporate America, and everything else. With a slant towards UNIX and Solaris, it gives great detail to operating systems to satisfy the most astute nerds, but offers enough broad range to reach anyone in the "office" world. **JOTD** is outrageously funny where humor doesn't even show itself – deep inside the world of Geekdom. And, **JOTD** isn't just a compilation of wimpy one-liners, but a collection of full-length caustic satires, zany scripts, and mature material. But, it is not *too* obscene, because the author once worked as a rabbi, and apparently even *he* has his limits.

What other book makes fun of the Korn Shell and Solaris' implementation of ksh, and does so while throwing in subtle references to celibacy and marriage? And, while UNIX shells might be a tad too esoteric for a general audience, **JOTD** topics such as making fun of dot com start-ups and employment recruiters are ones which most readers can relate to. **JOTD** makes fun of everything and everybody in the computer field: the hardware, the software, those who write the software, those who own the companies which produce it, those consumers who buy it, those stores which sell it, and those admins who have to install it on computers. And, although each joke has some sort of connection to the computer field, the satires are often pointed at politicians, entertainers, and well-known celebrities. Everyone with a sense of humor who either works within or has spent time in the world of technology, or has merely heard of technology, will enjoy and consider buying this book. And, it will make a perfect gift for the holiday season – after all, what kind of fun is receiving *"DOS for Dummies"* as a holiday present? Good grief. We can already hear the disappointment. We can already hear the cries, "where's my **JOTD**!?! I want my **JOTD**!!".

JOTD is a much-anticipated and long-awaited publication. That's right. In fact, there is already a JOTD Fan Club with a long list of members. So, the point is that scores of **JOTD** fans waited anxiously for the published collection of this geek comedy genius to become available.

Does **JOTD** have competition? Not really. The book and its author are totally innovative, original, and unique. There are other geek humor books out there on the shelves, but they are all wimpy material such as *"Dilbert"*. And, with enough fanfare, **JOTD** will outsell any humor book out there, because **JOTD** is hard hitting and outrageous. And, you ask:

>   What does JOTD stand for?
>
>   How did JOTD become the name of this book?
>
>   Why do I always get stuck reading these agonizing Forewords?
>
>   Is this Goldstein chick always this annoying?
>
>   Where did I leave my keys?
>
>   Has anyone seen my keys?
>
>   What the heck will I do if I can't find my keys?

Now, let us answer some of those questions: **JOTD** is an abbreviation for Joke Of The Day.

Did I mention that the author wrote all of these jokes while he was working as a UNIX network administrator? In UNIX, there is a file named "motd", which stands for Message Of The Day. Along the same lines, he decided to call each joke he wrote "jotd", standing for *Joke Of The Day*.

The author disseminated his jokes on the Internet each day by emailing them to members of his "JOTD" distribution address list – and he distributed the jokes one day at a time. A large percentage of the members of the JOTD** list are familiar with the world of computers in general and familiar with the world of UNIX in particular. As you will see in this book, many of the jotds are UNIX and computer network-related, but one need not be a member of IT (Information Technology) nor does one need to be a nerd or a geek to laugh at all of the jotds – one merely needs to laugh at all of the jotds.

Some of the material in this book is so specific to UNIX that I doubt anyone outside of Geekdom will understand it. Some of the material is so weird that even the author doesn't understand it. And, some of the material just plain old stinks. But, I'm sure you will find that much of the material is relevant to you or your work, is easily understandable, and best of all, low in fat and cholesterol.

By choosing only the BEST of his jokes, the author spared us all from having to read the really lousy stuff he created. We can all thank him for that later.

By the time you finish reading this book, you will know more about computers, UNIX, and Solaris than do most Microsoft experts. And you will probably know more about Microsoft than most Microsoft experts, which is odd, because this book is not even about Microsoft.

** Note: JOTD and jotd are interchangeable. Rabbs is hassle-free.

Now, here are some terms you will need to know the definitions of before you read **JOTD**:

TERM	DEFINITION

rabbi — a house if you are lucky

network – more than one computer connected electronically

computer – you are kidding me. You don't know what a computer is?

admin — administrator. Person who manages the computer network.

SUN – also can be Sun or Sun Microsystems. A company which makes computers which run on Solaris.

Solaris – one of the most respected flavors of UNIX.

UNIX – a high-tech operating system which has nothing to do with the ability to have children.

operating system – the software which runs the computer

software – coded programs written by geeks

OS – abbreviation for operating system

Windows – an inferior OS marketed by Microsoft

NT – (see Windows)

M$ — short for Microsoft.

Microsoft – the monopoly which forces its inferior operating system on the public.

See? This book is not only funny, but educational as well.

Signed,

Rachel Goldstein, UNIX Administrator.

Acknowledgements

I must thank the members of my JOTD distribution list for their continued support and encouragement. And, I must similarly thank the UNIX Users Association of Southern California, the most "kickin' it" user group around, whose members composed most of the original people on my JOTD list. It was in UUASC that I practiced my joke-writing craft and where my bizarre humor was always popular. I especially thank longtime JOTD supporters O'Shaughnessy Evans and Brian Mann who both archived all of my jokes from Day 1 of JOTD, making it really easy to create this book. And, a special thanks to Deirdre Saoirse, JOTD's first member who signed up within 60 seconds after the first announcement that the list was created.

I must also thank a number of ex-girlfriends — not by name, of course, (I don't want to get sued) — who desired to see my JOTDs published and gave me the idea to create this book. But, it was my first comedy coach who finally got my rear into gear to actually make **JOTD** happen in published form. Yes, I had a comedy coach. She charged thousands of dollars. She is the funny and talented Pattie Pica, who wears a short, black skirt — I'd like to take a Pica under her skirta – now, THAT would be worth thousands of dollars.

Thanks, Pattie.

Lastly, I must thank my young and beautiful assistant, Alexandra Thomas, without whose dedicated service, this book would never have been published.

If you would like to sign up for the unixrabbi's world famous **FREE** JOTD mailing list and receive jokes, please contact me at: **unixrabbi@rabbs.com** .

Did I mention that I do stand-up comedy? If you would like to see Rabbs perform in person, and want the dates and times of shows in your area, please contact me at: **unixrabbi@rabbs.com**.

If you would like the names of Rabbs' ex-girlfriends, please contact me at: **unixrabbi@rabbs.com** .

If you would like the phone number of my young and beautiful assistant, please contact me at: **unixrabbi@rabbs.com** .

And, if you would like to pica under Pattie's skirta, please contact me at: **unixrabbi@rabbs.com** .

Did I mention I have a big ego?

Did I mention I have my own website?

Check out my big ego at my website, **www.rabbs.com**

Did I mention I used to work as a rabbi? (can you believe that?)

Did I mention I wrote a book?

Check out my book by flipping this page.

JOTD is a crack up. But, don't take the author's word for it. Take a look at a sample of the humor by viewing a few jotds already archived on the Internet, and pay attention to what other geeks are saying about them at:

    www.rabbs.com/jokes.html

    Signed,

    Rabbs

What's Inside —
with Joke Titles

Note: The method of arranging the book into specific chapters was based on grouping
jokes into logical sets based on commonality, in an order that made sense.
However, there is nothing "holy" about the ordering of chapters, of the ordering of
jokes within chapters, or the amount of chapters, or the pairings of jokes to chapters. In fact, there is nothing holy at all about this book. JOTD does not claim to
represent any religious denomination whatsoever, and the author takes pride in
knowing that no harm was caused to any animal in the publication of this material.

Chapter 1

THE JOB SEARCH

How To Write a Cover Letter

Hello,

I am a UNIX network administrator who is extremely interested in the position I saw posted on the Internet. I believe my work experiences make me a perfect match for your company. Let me explain why:

I am looking for a Fortune 500 firm like yours, and not some start-up web site, where everyone has to kill themselves working so hard just so the company can survive. I don't want to work long hours. I am cut out for the corporate USA average of 5.3 hours of work per day (a generous estimate) spread out over a 40 hour week, where I am never more than 15 minutes from a coffee break and 50 feet from the water cooler. I need to be working for a company which won't depend on me 24 x 7, won't need me in times of crisis, and will hire me as a member of a team large enough so that coverage and responsibility is so spread out amongst the team members that no one has to do anything more substantial than just show up to work and belch.

I need to be working for a firm that is so huge and financially secure that money is never an object when determining salaries, bonuses, number of employees, and workloads. Your company is clearly one of those places where I can be set up with a corner office and never be bothered again until I retire, where no one will care if I don't do anything more productive during my entire tenure than figure out how to adjust the building's thermostat, and yet, I will enjoy salary increases on a annual basis. Basically, I am looking for what your ad described as a "corporate welfare" position, where your firm will be providing me with a place to go every day and make me feel like I have something to do and offer the world, where I will be taken care of financially, and where I can still have time at work to tend to my personal duties as well.

The personal duties area is where I definitely qualify, having just broken several employee records for handling personal matters at my present place of employment, including:

• Most photocopies for personal use produced in a month (25,000)

• Most long distance phone call hours produced in one month (36)

• Most hours spent in one day surfing the Internet (9.5) Note: We only work an 8 hour day!

• Most personal emails sent via company email in one day (205)

• Most faxes sent for personal use in one month (630)

• Most total hours in one month spent in restroom reading (30)

Clearly, I am a perfect fit for your company. Please call me at work (where I am sure I can make some time for your phone call) ASAP to discuss the opportunities for me at your firm. I look forward to your call.

Sincerely,

UNIX Admin

Actual Conversations with Headhunters

Monday

UNIX admin:	"If I wouldn't leave my job two weeks ago when you called offering $90K, why would I leave now for $70K?"
Headhunter:	"This is a position that was made for you. I have 100 other candidates I could call, but you are the one I really want to place."
UNIX admin:	"Why are you calling me at work?"
Headhunter:	"Because you got mad when I called you at home"
UNIX admin:	(Hmmm…that makes sense. If someone gets angry when you call them in one place, see if they are any less angry when you call them again in another place) "How did you get this phone number?"
Headhunter:	"I saw your résumé posted on the web"
UNIX admin:	"You mean the one that says at the top of it, *'Recruiters, please note: I am not actively seeking employment at this time'*?"

Headhunter:	"Oh, you're not available. Let me ask you a question. I don't have anyone else to call. Do you know anyone else who might want this job?"

Tuesday

Headhunter:	"I just read your résumé and I have a position that is perfect for you. It is for a computer operator at a Fortune 500 company, and it pays $14 per hour. Isn't that amazing?"
UNIX admin:	"Yes. It is amazing you can say you read my résumé!"

Wednesday

Headhunter:	"I would like you to interview for a data entry position at a law office."
UNIX admin:	"Excuse me?"
Headhunter:	"The best part of this job is that you'll be working with lawyers, so its perfect if you ever want to be a paralegal."
UNIX admin:	"Why would I want to go into the legal profession? To be able to sue you for ruining my career?"

Thursday

Solaris admin:	"I just interviewed at the company you sent me to"

Headhunter:	"I know, they already called me and said they are very interested in you"
Solaris admin:	"Really? I told them I couldn't accept the position and walked out"
Headhunter:	"But, it is a Solaris job with an opportunity to learn NT"
Solaris admin:	"No, its an NT job with a chance to learn SGI. They have 100 NT boxes and two Silicon Graphics machines. Why do you call it a Solaris job?"
Headhunter:	"They said it was SGI, and I thought that stood for Solaris something."

Friday

Headhunter:	"I have your résumé in front of me and I think you match the following opportunity: It pays $80 per hour, its all Solaris, blah, blah, blah, blah, blah."
Solaris jr. admin:	"How much experience is required?"
Headhunter:	"10 years minimum"
Solaris jr. admin:	"Well, while my résumé is in front of you, why don't you read it?"

Week Two

Monday

UNIX admin:	"I just got laid off, so I am on the market. I'd like to fax to you my résumé for your database."
Headhunter:	"Don't bother us right now. We don't have any UNIX listings, and I don't have time to deal with your résumé"

Seven days later

Same headhunter:	"Hi, how are you? OK, I have a hot opportunity that just arrived in UNIX, but I must have your résumé NOW!!"
UNIX admin:	"Wait a minute, when I needed you, you treated me like chopped liver. Now that you need me, you say you need my résumé NOW!?! Maybe I'm too busy now to fax it"
Headhunter:	"You HAVE to fax it, because you don't have a choice since you need a job"
UNIX admin:	"Wrong. You waited too long to call me. I was hired somewhere yesterday. And, I start tomorrow."
Headhunter:	"Doesn't matter. Just fax your résumé. This job is better than the one you accepted."
UNIX admin:	"Pardon me, but how could you possibly know that?"
Headhunter:	"This job is hot"

UNIX admin:	"What is it?"
Headhunter:	"It is for a top-notch C++ and UNIX developer"
UNIX admin:	"Those are two things I know nothing about"
Headhunter:	"But, you wanted a UNIX job"
UNIX admin:	"This proves you should have let me fax to you my résumé last week so that you could read that I am an admin. Perhaps I should still fax it to you so that you will have it for future reference."
Headhunter:	"No reason to now. You'll be working at your new job for a while, so I don't need it."

Seven days later

Same headhunter:	"I need you to fax ASAP, I have a UNIX admin job for you"

The next Wednesday

Headhunter:	"I have a good job for you, but let me ask you a question first. How much money are you presently making?
UNIX admin:	"I might be interested in the job, but let me ask you a question first. How much moneyare YOU presently making?"
Headhunter:	"Your question isn't pertinent to this conversation"

UNIX admin: "Your question isn't pertinent to this conversation"

Headhunter: "But if you answer my question right, I can place you at this company"

UNIX admin: "If you answer my question right, I might use you to represent me to this company"

The next day

Female headhunter   "I have a good job for you, but let me ask you a question first. How much money are you presently making?

Male UNIX admin: "I might be interested in the job, but let me ask you a question first. What are you wearing right now?"

Female headhunter   "That's none of your business! I will ignore that and ask you again, how much money are you presently making?"

Male UNIX admin: "That's none of your business! I will ignore that and ask you again, what are you wearing right now?"

Female headhunter   "Fine. I am wearing a black mini-dress and high heels. Now, how much money are you presently making?"

Male UNIX admin: "Enough to take you out to dinner. "

Two weeks later

Headhunter: "One of my clients has a need for a new admin. The present Solaris admin guy has well, let things go.

Backups aren't being done. The system crashed and was restored with a two-year-old restore. "

UNIX admin:

"Question: What the hell was the admin doing there all day if he wasn't doing backups, etc? Was he:

a) flirting with female headhunters on the phone?
b) emailing jokes to various lists?
c) schmoozing with his girlfriend on the phone?
d) surfing the Net in search of porno?
e) performing stand-up comedy for his co-workers?
f) more than one of the above?
g) all of the above?
h) none of the above?
i) how do I apply for the job?"

The Interview

UNIX admin:

"Hi, I just left work early and drove two hours for my appointment to interview with one of your recruiters. His name is Alan and he described what I consider the perfect UNIX admin opportunity for me, which is why I actually took off from work for this interview. I rarely do this."

Headhunter:

"Alan doesn't work here anymore. We have no records of anyone making an appointment for this evening with us. We close in five minutes, and no one is available to stay late for you. And, even if we could, we don't have any UNIX admin listings right now. Now you know why Alan doesn't work here anymore."

The Headhunter Countdown

10 The number of times each day the headhunter will call you once a company makes you an offer.

9 The number of thousands of dollars the offer is short by.

8 The number of times in one conversation that the headhunter will tell you that no one is going to give you the money you are holding out for, even though he or she without hesitation submitted your résumé all over town knowing exactly what your salary requirements are.

7 The number of times during negotiations that the headhunter will tell you that the company you presently work for is going nowhere, and therefore you should accept any other offer. And, of course, one would think that he or she should know that, because he or she just placed three people at your company.

6 The number of days in a row should you accept the offer that the headhunter will ask you if you submitted your letter of resignation yet.

5 The number of times in one conversation you will hear how the best company to work for is a Fortune 500 firm or a startup website, depending on which one the headhunter is trying to convince you to join this time.

4 The amount of times each day should you accept the offer that the headhunter will warn you not to entertain a counter-offer from your boss.

3 The amount of thousands of dollars the headhunter is willing to chip in from their own commission to entice you into taking the job you've been offered but don't want.

2 The amount of times each day after you start working at the new job, should you accept the offer, that the headhunter will tell you to keep working there at least 3 months before leaving, no matter how much you realize you made a bad decision in accepting the position, because "things tend to get better after a few months". Interesting that the headhunter only gets paid if you stay 90 days.

1 The number of times per phone message left on your answering machine by the headhunter saying that this is a perfect match between you and the company which made the offer $9K too short, and that he or she wants to make both parties happy by reaching an agreement, when in reality, the headhunter couldn't give a hoot about either party, and only cares about his or her own commission sliding away.

0 The number of times the headhunter will return your phone calls after your interview until an offer is made. From that point on, go back to number 10 and repeat the countdown.

Actual Conversations with Headhunters Part II

Headhunter:	"I have an opening at a hot new company called Start-up.website.com."
UNIX admin:	"How much can they pay?"
Headhunter:	"They don't have a lot of money yet because they are only a start-up, but they can offer stock options. Their stock is going to soar."
UNIX admin:	"How much can they pay?"
Headhunter:	"I will have to find out. Meanwhile, I have an opening at a hot new company called IPO.start-up.website.com."
UNIX admin:	"How much can they pay?"
Headhunter:	"I am not sure if they can pay competitively yet, but they can offer a lot in stock options instead. But, their stock hasn't moved yet."
UNIX admin:	"How much can they pay?"
Headhunter:	"I will have to find out. Meanwhile, I have an opening at a hot new company called Pre-IPO.start-up.website.com."

UNIX admin: "How much can they pay?"

Headhunter: "They are well funded and about to go on the market. They should be able to offer you stock then, possibly in lieu of high pay, and one day, that stock might be worth something."

UNIX admin: "How much can they pay?"

Headhunter: "I will have to find out. Meanwhile, I have an opening at a hot new company called VC.pre-IPO.start-up.website.com."

UNIX admin: "How much can they pay?"

Headhunter: "They have some funding but will have to pay you everything in stocks but they won't be going public for a while. Their stock isn't going to be worth much. This company is close to bankruptcy."

UNIX admin: "In other words, they all pay the same."

Dot Comedies

I know not to buy stock in one of those dot com start-ups. You know which ones I am talking about — they started with names like hotopportunity.com and guar-anteedtomakemoney.com, and, of course, my favorite, evenbetterthansex.com . But, they all lost money and are going out of business, and now have names like failure.com, and massivefailure.com, and of course, totallyscrewed.com. That is why I call them dot comedies. AND I COINED THAT TERM LONG BEFORE A TV SHOW AIRED BY THAT NAME.

Start-ups all use a lot of hyped terminology. Dot comedies talk about stock options, rounds of funding, and going IPO. Let us call those terms what they really are –

"Stock options" = shares of worthless equity

"Competitive salary" = less than market rate

"first round of funding" = someone gave us two dollars

"well-funded" = haven't turned a dime yet

"pre-IPO" = venture capitalists want out of this dead duck ASAP

"e-commerce" = e-bust

More Dot Comedies

QUESTION: What's the difference between being paid in stocks from a start-up Internet company and being paid in Monopoly money from the player controlling the bank?

ANSWER: At least the value of the Monopoly money won't drop.

ANSWER: You can buy a hotel on Boardwalk with the Monopoly money.

ANSWER: The value of the Boardwalk hotel won't drop.

What to Say to a Dot Comedy

Before accepting a position at a start-up, remember to:

ask them what their cash-burn rate is

ask them if they have enough funding to last through August

ask them how long they realistically expect to stay in business

ask them how many shares of worthless equity they will promise you

ask them if they are B to B, B to C, or just another D- to F

ask them if they are planning to work you 24 hours per day and then want you to work nights as well

ask them what their business model is, and if it is to generate money via Internet advertising, you are not interested

ask them if they plan to turn over their entire management 14 times per year, so you can bet that the people who interviewed you will not be there once you are hired

And of course,

ask them if their ultimate goal is to spend their final $1 million in a last-ditch effort to stay in business by buying an ad in the Super Bowl, only to find out that by the time the game starts, they can no longer afford the $35 annual domain name registration fee, and therefore, by halftime, you can't even view their web site.

Chapter 2

At Work

Internal Memorandum

Date: May 1, 2004

SUBJECT: UNIX team status report for the week.

Accomplished This Week:

We were a little slow on the delivery of the 10 requested fully installed and configured brand new workstations, but we did manage to accomplish the following:

1) Jimmy picked up the discount movie tickets from the company store as his girlfriend requested.

2) Ray finally photocopied his tax forms on the IT Xerox machine as his wife has nagged him to do for weeks.

3) Cheryl redecorated her cubicle with the paraphernalia she bought at the Dodgers game.

4) Louis spent a lot of time on the phone calling different plumbers but eventually nailed one down who could come to his place when he is home at night.

5) Ashley finally got through on the phone to the cable company to argue her bill and order HBO.

With everything going on, we did not miss:

a single coffee break, cigarette, nor lunch out together

exchanging jokes emailed to us from our friends in cyberspace

surfing the Net on a daily basis

writing emails to our families

playing the latest game which Jimmy installed on our computers

Plans for Next Week:

1) Jimmy needs to hook up with the head of accounting to explain why circumstances beyond our control are causing the delay in the delivery of the workstations

2) Ray needs to hook up with the head of accounting as well to discuss whether they are going to buy Lakers playoff tickets together or not, and try to figure out who is going to win the NBA title this year

3) Cheryl needs to speak with her boyfriend on the phone all next week to determine where "they are going" in their relationship

4) Louis needs to take off early a couple of times next week while no one is looking so that he can be at home for the plumber

5) Ashley is very upset with the latest bill from her doctor and will spend much of next week on the phone arguing with the doctor's business office about it.

I Know that I am a Senior UNIX Admin When...

I spend the whole day on the phone talking with my girlfriend.

I know all of the best looking women in the next building.

I run the most powerful systems in the industry, but the computer on my desk is the weakest one on the planet.

I wear a beeper just to look cool, but the other admins on my team actually respond to their pages.

The rest of the team arrives at work early in the morning when it is still dark outside and leaves when it is already dark at night, I come to work when it is warm outside and leave when no one is looking.

The first thing the rest of the team does when arriving is read system email and check the logs, I rush in to read my personal email and check my stocks.

The rest of the team uses Netscape to bookmark on-line documentation, I use it to bookmark important sites like weather maps, surf reports, and traffic updates.

The rest of the team works, I take all of the credit.

I spend the whole day on the phone with headhunters so that I can determine my market value.

I know who in the industry is looking for a new job so that I can get a referral fee when speaking with headhunters.

The rest of the team is writing shell scripts and programs, I write jokes and email to lists.

The only programs I ever write are Trojan Horses to pull pranks on other teammates and users.

The only printer I rush to fix is the local one that I use to print incoming jokes.

I am a whiz on the latest video game I loaded on my pc.

I take two-hour lunches and tell everyone I was fixing a computer in Building 3 during the first hour.

I realize hours spent involved in skiing, tennis, surfing, and basketball are all counted towards the 40-hour minimum workweek.

I keep my teammates from reporting my activities to management by convincing them that they need me, because I am the one who can convince management not to dump the UNIX network in favor of NT.

Probably the only thing I do that even resembles work is fighting management on the NT vs. UNIX thing, and that is not even part of my job description.

I am the first in line at the company cafeteria when I choose to eat lunch at work.

I tell my teammates I am fixing a crisis in Building 4 only five minutes after I hear that someone is giving away free doughnuts in Building 4.

And, finally, I know that I am a senior UNIX admin when:

I arrive at work just before lunch time, read my email, and go home right after everyone comes back.

Question: How many UNIX Admins does it take...?

QUESTION: How many Unix Admins does it take to change a light bulb?

ANSWER: Two. One to put a new bulb in and one to convince management that the light bulb idea shouldn't be scrapped just because one blew out.

•••

QUESTION: How many NT admins does it take to change a light bulb?

ANSWER: None. All you have to do instead is turn off and on the power switch every half of an hour.

•••

QUESTION: How many AppleTalk admins does it take to change a light bulb?

ANSWER: Three. One to change your bulb, one to super-size your fries, and one to ask if you want paper or plastic.

An Admin's Wish List

Dear Santa,

I hope all is well on the North Pole. I made a list of what I want this year. Here it is:

• a web site in which Java adds value to the pages rather than just slowing them down

• one honest man in Redmond or in Washington D.C. (either one is fine, Santa)

• a woman to date who doesn't think I am castrated when I say I'm a UNIX guy

• non-geek friends who aren't befuddled when I tell them I know nothing about how to fix their PC's and Windows problems

• not having to explain to the novice that an admin isn't a programmer and isn't a technician (hmmm.....what *do* we do?)

• a scanner vendor who doesn't ask me if Solaris runs on a Mac or Windows

• after answering "what do you do for a living?" with "UNIX network administrator" the other person doesn't have that glossed over face looking like Bambi gazing into headlights

• after answering that same question with "computer guy", I don't have to hear about Excel and spreadsheets

• after answering "run a computer network" I don't hear "oh, is that an on-line dating service?"

• after answering "systems administrator" I don't hear "military or space systems?"

—and, finally, my favorite:

Santa, I know it is difficult, but please give me the ability to avoid the following conversation:

After answering "computer specialist", I hear:

— "what do you specialize in?"

"UNIX"

—"what's that?"

"a high tech operating system"

—"is that like Windows?"

"no, I said it was high tech"

—"can I get UNIX?"

"sure, what apps do you want to run?"

—"Word, Outlook, PowerPoint"

"I doubt UNIX can help you"

—"so much for it being high tech"

Top 10 Reasons IT Department Meetings are Like Senate Debates

10 Never scheduled at a convenient time.

9 The popular decision is never the right decision.

8 A number of perfunctory votes are taken that don't have any long-term effect.

7 Those who are opposed to the idea of meetings see no positive gain in continuing to hold them, while those in favor of them continue to schedule them even though its obvious nothing will change.

6 You can't get rid of the person in power.

5 It is non-stop lies and rhetoric.

4 Jews are vastly outnumbered, yet, they make the most noise.

3 90% of the time is spent searching for a way to adjourn to get back to work.

2 The only time everyone is awake is when a speaker is

cracking jokes.

And, finally, the no. 1 reason IT Dept. meetings are like Senate debates:

1   You can never find even one attractive woman to stare at.

Drawbacks to working in the field of computers

The biggest downside to working in IT I have found so far is that I have to sit in a cubicle. And, when I sit in a cubicle, I have to listen to the guy in the next cubicle make disgusting noises all day long every day. It gets so bad that I end up counting and tallying his various noises. Yesterday, he broke his record by clearing his throat 27 times, plus he had two burps and a cough.

I got back at him by farting.

Eerie Similarities between Secretaries and Admins

Secretaries' Day	one day per year everyone kisses their butt
Admins' day	one Sunday per month, admin kisses his weekend good-bye to work on network, no buts
Secretaries' Week	one week of free lunches
Admins' week	"there are no free lunches as we have one week to get this network upgraded"
secretaries	type pages
admins	answer pages
secretaries	run to get coffee
admins	get to run Java
secretaries	Prozac
admins	caffeine
secretaries	go nuts
admins	doughnuts
secretaries	work whole day while bored
admins	whole day on Internet watching their stock drop on Big Board

secretaries	clueless around admins when it comes to their own computer
admins	clueless around secretaries when it comes to typing a simple memo
secretaries	lean over desk and turn on powerful men
admins	lean over desk and turn on power switches

Chapter 3

Software, Women, and Other Sports

Eerie similarities between Solaris and NT

Solaris	so good that journals can't stop raving about it
NT	so good that M$ marketing team can't stop raving about it

Solaris	unlock screen saver every 30 minutes
NT	boot every 30 minutes

Solaris	boot every few months
NT	re-install every few months

Solaris	re-install with every OS upgrade
NT	4,000 new bugs with every OS upgrade

Solaris	64 bits
NT	not worth two bits

Solaris	endless task by McNealy
NT	endless tasks brings it to its kneelies

Solaris	"Network is the Computer"
NT	"Network hoses this Computer"

Solaris	disable DT and log in from blue screen
NT	kill a process and receive Blue Screen of Death

Solaris	handles files as big as 9 million terabytes
NT	handle it gently or it makes terrible bites

| Solaris | schleps files out of your swap |
| NT | schleps gelt out of your wallet |

| Solaris | dependable |
| NT | expendable |

| Solaris | runs 24/7 |
| NT | runs for about 24 minutes 7 seconds |

| Solaris | compares to 18-wheeler moving your furniture |
| NT | if you chain 25 Geo Metros together, and each one takes a pillow and a lamp… |

| Solaris | a simple DNS |
| NT | a sample of PMS |

| Solaris | 100% Pure Java |
| NT | 100% Pure Hell |

| Solaris | multi-tasking/multi-threaded/ 2 to the 16th power processes |
| NT | don't touch that mouse!, you'll hose it! |

| Solaris | cron jobs |
| NT | con job |

| Solaris | Legato |
| NT | Win 20 - uh - oh!! |

| Solaris | the crux of high tech |
| NT | from crooks of high crime |

Solaris	favorite of famous sys admins
NT	favorite of infamous sissy managers
Solaris	costs dough, but its worth what you pay for it
NT	costs nothing, and you get what you pay for
Solaris	caches in swap
NT	might get your cash back in a swap
Solaris	study it for weeks and get certified
NT	what do you have to know? Ctrl-Alt-Del? here's your certificate
Solaris	monitors RAM
NT	bleeds RAM
Solaris	DES bundled
NT	security bumbled
Solaris	features Hot Java
NT	OS takes coffee break
Solaris	inetd is mother of all daemons
NT	Bill G. is father of all demons
Solaris	forks new processes
NT	put a fork in it, that process is done
Solaris	drivers communicate with the PROM
NT	its users need drivers to the prom
Solaris	you get grep, awk, and sed
NT	you get DOS, enough said!

| Solaris | NFS, NIS, NIS+, RPC |
| NT | me too |

| Solaris | one server handles thousands of power users |
| NT | one screen shows hundreds of cryptic icons |

| Solaris | system can be managed by a joke writer |
| NT | a joke the way the system managed to be written |

| Solaris | old versions still hang around corporate world |
| NT | just hangs |

| Solaris | works around the clock while admins work about 8 hours a day |
| NT | works about 8 hours a day while admins work around the clock |

| Solaris | NIS+ protects against snoopers, so who needs insecure Gates? |
| NT | monopoly protects against market shift, so who needs OS security fences? |

| Solaris | one admin, many terminals situated surrounding him |
| NT | many admins, one terminal situation surrounding them |

| Solaris | must know how to use the tools |
| NT | must have tools to tweak the How |

| Solaris | binaries allow unlimited use |
| NT | overuse corrupts binaries |

Solaris	tested
NT	toasted

Solaris	download patches
NT	a large load brings it down and requires patches

Solaris	from high atop Mountain View, and from down in Silicon Valley
NT	CPU is flat line

Solaris	huge directory trees
NT	belongs with the other toys under huge Christmas trees

And, finally,

Solaris	"Can't touch it"
NT	"Can't ping it"

Solaris and NT in a Nutshell

Question: What's the best way to transfer data between two computers running NT?

Answer: Re-install both machines with Solaris

I Just Saw the Following Ad to Buy Software

And, well, I got to thinking — how about an offer to program things that will really change my mood? Now, that might entice me into biting at the offer. I would like software that would launch:

1) a woman who cleans my house (I call it Maid 1.0)

2) a woman who does my shopping (I call it Servant 2.2)

3) a woman who handles my laundry (I call it Slave 3.1)

4) a woman who cooks my meals (I call it Personal Chef 4.0)

5) a woman who tells me how great I am (I call it Honey 5.2)

6) a woman who tells me how smart I am (I call it Sweetie 2.1)

7) a woman who tells me how cute I am (I call it Baby 1.3)

8) a woman who tells me how funny I am (I call it Lovey 3.0)

Now, I wonder if I can get that all bundled into one product? Hmmm...what would I call it? Well, I'd like to call it **Wife 1.0**, but that wouldn't work, because it wouldn't be portable. For instance, even if I installed it, the Jewish version wouldn't function the way it was supposed to, and would be price prohibitive to make it cover all eight requirements. And, even if it could eventually work properly, all of the re-writes would bring it to version 9.9.9 and require years of compiling before it was ready to be shrink-wrapped.

And, I am sure it would come with bugs like:

1) ERROR: eating disorder

2) ERROR: too many demands

3) ERROR: whining

4) ERROR: castrating

5) ERROR: only know from the word "no" in the bedroom

6) ERROR: what did user say wrong this time?

7) ERROR: user guilty of insufficient memory

8) ERROR: software always right, user always wrong

9) ERROR: Fatal: neurotic and repressed

10) ERROR: user in the doghouse again and doesn't know what he did wrong

11) ERROR: software is always right even when it is wrong…and user needs to understand that!

12) ERROR: system announced it was going to do something, and user didn't try to stop it

And, of course, the bug fixes are very expensive:

1) Yearly Trip to Hawaii 1.1

2) New Car 2.2

3) Remodeled Kitchen 2.1

4) Psychoanalyst 3.0

5) Marriage Counselor 3.1

6) Bigger House 2.1

7) Better Job 1.0

8) Better Job 1.1

9) Better Job 1.2

10) Better Job 1.3

11) Better Job 2.0

Hmmm…I guess settling for turning lights off and on doesn't seem so bad anymore.

Virus Alert

IT DEPARTMENT MANAGER VIRUS:

Acts like a daemon. Prevents old and dying processes, many of which are causing harm to the system, from being terminated. Meanwhile, it prevents new and innovative processes from starting. This is the mother virus, because with the wrong processes running, the system may contract the following:

MIKE TYSON VIRUS:

Chews up a big hunk of out of your Audio Tool.

DENNIS RODMAN VIRUS:

Strange colors and images appear on your screen, and then suddenly, your keyboard kicks you right in the groin.

STANLEY CUP PLAYOFFS VIRUS:

Your modem disconnects immediately after the handshaking event.

BASEBALL VIRUS:

You pay way too much for watered down versions of slow devices and fat sotware, only to have the whole thing refuse to work. Then, you go out and pay inflated prices, as much as 10 times more, to replace the hardware and software with even more watered down versions.

MONICA LEWINSKY VIRUS:

Allows data streams to input to the wrong port.

LINDA TRIPP VIRUS:

Backs up on tape your most confidential files even if you don't own a tape drive.

HILLARY CLINTON VIRUS:

Files disappear, only to mysteriously reappear a year later in another directory.

BILL CLINTON VIRUS:

During start-up self-test, things get confused and your floppy becomes a hard drive. This is common when the virus detects the Monica Lewinsky Virus present during the self-test.

Netscape vs. Internet Explorer

I have a confession to make. Actually, I have two confessions to make. First, I must confess that I haven't taken a shower in two days and it is getting a bit gamy inside this cubicle, and second, I must confess that I use Internet Explorer whenever possible, instead of using Netscape. Here are my Top 10 reasons for preferring Internet Explorer:

10 I can actually connect with more sites for some reason (that could be due to some sinister plot of Mr. Gates, though)

9 Netscape, both Communicator and Navigator, seems to freeze on me periodically, locking up the computer so bad that it forces me to re-boot as the only way to kill it

8 I get into M$ Hotmail faster with Internet Explorer (gee, wonder why?)

7 Internet Explorer prints from cache while Netscape goes back out to the web site when you tell it to print

6 Chicks dig IE

5 IE is easier to spell

4 Chicks dig being referred to as my "favorites" rather than as my "bookmarks"

3   Ego

2   Did I mention chicks?

And, of course, my number one reason for using Internet Explorer is:

1   You don't have to shower if you use Internet Explorer regularly

Korn Shell on Solaris

Solaris has never included any version of Korn Shell more recent than the 11/16/88 version, and Sun has no plans to ever bundle a more updated version with their OS.

That's really wonderful, because if you read "The New Kornshell Command and Programming Language", by David Korn, you will see on virtually every single page, sometimes more than once on a page, the following line:

"This feature is available only on versions of ksh newer than the 11/16/88 version."

If you insist on using ksh in Solaris, then I would say not to bother reading that book, because it is pretty worthless when you are on Solaris.

It is like for me reading manuals about different sexual techniques. I can sit there for hours on end studying and memorizing that stuff, but since I haven't had a partner since 11/16/88, I don't have any way to test the wild positions described. That's why I stay with csh.

I bet you didn't know that, btw. I bet you'd never guess the reason I use C Shell is because I haven't had anyone in bed since 11/16/88.

Now, some will argue that no one should ever use csh. I argue that no one should ever go this long without a sex partner. Maybe using csh is part of the reason why I'm not getting any. Maybe using csh is part of the reason I am going crazy and writing jokes like this for total strangers.

And, if you are going to say, "Rabbs, try out ksh, maybe you'll be surprised and get some" , I will counter by reminding you that I only have the old version of ksh, so even if I get lucky, I won't get all of the good stuff - you know — no this, no that, no the other, just a lot of "no" in the bedroom. Funny though, a lot of friends of mine who are married to Jewish women tell me that that is all they're getting right now, themselves, anyway. Hmm, maybe they are also all running an old version of ksh.

(which lead us to……..Chapter 4 ….)

Chapter 4

Trying to Capture the Jewish Market

Jewish vs. Geek Weddings

I have been asked to perform a wedding between two computer geeks. In preparing for this awesome event, I am finding many differences between it and traditional Jewish weddings I am used to, such as:

Jewish wedding	separate seating, one section for men, one for women
Geek wedding	separate seating, one section for the Mac crowd, one for the Windows crowd, one for the UNIX crowd, while the BeOS crowd has to stand
Jewish wedding	man gives his bride a token ring
Geek wedding	everyone on a Token Ring
Jewish wedding	the mothers get together and break a dish
Geek wedding	the mothers Telnet via a satellite dish
Jewish wedding	set up a Chupah (wedding canopy)
Geek wedding	set up an X Windows session
Jewish wedding	bride's father is the host
Geek wedding	bride's workstation is the xhost
Jewish wedding	bride wears white
Geek wedding	depends on your graphics card
Jewish wedding	couple doesn't touch until after the wedding
Geek wedding	couple touches files the moment they log on

Jewish wedding	the man draws a sip of flowing wine and breaks the glass
Geek wedding	the man draws a flowchart and breaks the code

Jewish wedding	before the reception, the newlyweds are alone in a room
Geek wedding	if there is poor reception from your cable modem, you are the one alone in a room

Jewish wedding	newlyweds always late to reception, so guests in the mean time served coffee
Geek wedding	guests always late, so reception live on web for those with real time Java

Jewish wedding	don't even consider going if you plan to find a date
Geek wedding	don't even consider finding a date unless you want to go to a Star Trek convention

Jewish wedding	everyone dances and tries to entertain the newlyweds
Geek wedding	you entertain yourself with Quake and Freecell waiting for this night to end

and finally,

Jewish wedding	the rabbi charges big bucks to do basically nothing
Geek wedding	the rabbi charges big bucks to do virtually nothing

Jews vs. Geeks/Geeks vs. Jews

Jews vs. Geeks:

Chanukah commemorates the triumph over the Greeks.
The Web signifies the triumph of the Geeks.

Jews	live for the Sabbath on Friday night and Saturdays
Geeks	live for shopping at Fry's at night and on Saturdays
Jews	burn candles on Friday nights
Geeks	burn CDs on Friday nights
Jews	familiar with bar mitzvahs
Geeks	familiar with #bar -mtzv ahs
Jews	always looking for a bargain and know the price of everything they are into
Geeks	MicroTimes, Computer Currents, Data Comm Warehouse, Workstation Express, and Sunserver; ads from Best Buy, Egghead, CompUSA, Staples, and Fry's; not to mention 100 bookmarked web sites
Jews	everyone has "the" synagogue they won't go to
Geeks	everyone has "the" system they can't port to
Jews	10 kids in a mini-van
Geeks	10 cards in a mini-tower

Jews	adjust their skullcaps
Geeks	tweak their termcaps
Jews	everyone living in your neighborhood knows your name
Geeks	everyone working in your local Fry's knows your name
Jews	everyone nags you to find a nice boy/girl and settle down
Geeks	everyone bugs you to find a nice platform and settle down
Jews	wrap their arm with Tefillin
Geeks	wrap their arm with SCSI cables

Geeks vs. Jews:

2 Geeks, 3 computers
2 Jews, 3 opinions

Geeks	know about interrupts
Jews	know how to interrupt
Geeks	rehash everything to make it run right
Jews	rehash everything to prove they are right
Geeks	know how to push maps
Jews	know how to push through crowds, but can't read maps
Geeks	make up for coming in late by leaving late
Jews	make up for coming in late by leaving early

| Geeks | everyone talks about Y2K and dates in the future |
| Jews | everyone asks you why you aren't married, but no one finds you dates for the future |

| Geeks | find a URL through Netcenter, Excite, and Yahoo! |
| Jews | find a dollar in the Met Center, get excited, and shout "yahoo!" |

| Geeks | have other people's personal computers configured |
| Jews | have other people's personal lives all figured |

| Geeks | want to know everything about rdate |
| Jews | want to know everything about our date |

| Geeks | know grep comes from sed |
| Jews | know greps comes from gas |

(greps is a burp in Yiddish)

and finally,

| Geeks | with long beards and glasses they look like Jews |
| Jews | with long beards and ties they look like total geeks |

Jewish vs. Geek Weddings Part II

Geek wedding   everyone is given a choice of Cheetos or
                      M&M's, and served caffeinated beverages, and yet,
                      everyone feels at home.

Jewish wedding   everyone is given a choice of prime rib or
                      fish, and served alcoholic beverages, and yet, everyone
                      complains.

It took longer to decide which wedding was the punch line than it took to write the joke.

Chapter 5

Unix Songs

Yellow Subroutine

In a function where I got stuck,
Was a reserved name I had not seen,
And it acted as a system call causing a sequence of subroutines.
So I ran it and it output colors and finally froze my screen
And now my monitor shines like a banana, frozen in my yellow subroutine.

My screen's stuck in a yellow subroutine,
Yellow subroutine,
Yellow subroutine,
My screen's stuck in a yellow subroutine,
Yellow subroutine,
Yellow subroutine.

And I wonder how much memory is stored,
Watching my computer I soon get bored,
What's all the delay?

My screen's stuck in a yellow subroutine,
Yellow subroutine,
Yellow subroutine,
My screen's stuck in a yellow subroutine,
Yellow subroutine,
Yellow subroutine.

Suddenly something happened not foreseen,
Some of the color turned to green.
Lines of blue appeared on my screen,
In my yellow subroutine.

My screen's stuck in a yellow subroutine,
Yellow subroutine,
Yellow subroutine,
My screen's stuck in a yellow subroutine,
Yellow subroutine,
Yellow subroutine.

My screen's stuck in a yellow subroutine,
Yellow subroutine,
Yellow subroutine,
My screen's stuck in a yellow subroutine,
Yellow subroutine,
Yellow subroutine.

A Hard Disk Night

It's been a hard disk night
And I've wiped out all of your work in cronlog
It's been a hard disk night
I should kill all of your bg jobs
But when I ftp> get $HOME of you
I snoop the work that you do
Then you will realize my might

You know I hack all day
They pay me money to run their app
And it's worth it just to hear them say
You know our system runs like crap

So why I love to be root
'Cause I don't give a hoot
I'm the admin from hell

When I'm root everyone seems to be scared
When I'm root everyone knows I don't care, care, yeah

It's been a hard disk night
And I've wiped out all of your work in cronlog
It's been a hard disk night
I should kill all of your bg jobs
But when I ftp> get $HOME of you
I snoop the work that you do
Then you will realize my might

JOTD

So why I love to be root
'Cause I don't give a hoot
I'm the admin from hell

When I'm root everyone seems to be scared
When I'm root everyone knows I don't care, care, yeah

It's been a hard disk night
And I've wiped out all of your work in cronlog
It's been a hard disk night
I should kill all of your bg jobs
But when I ftp> get $HOME of you
I snoop the work that you do
Then you will realize my might

I know you feel my might
I know you feel my might

Chapter 6

How to Post Email to Unix Users Groups

How to Introduce Yourself to the User Group

When asked to introduce myself to the group, here is what I answer with:

"Hi folks. My name is Hershel Remer, but you may call me Rabbs, and I am celebrating a lifetime of dating unstable Jewish chicks who don't put out. I am a rabbi, a UNIX admin, a comic, a surfer, I have a really big ego, and on occasion, I wear women's panties. What I don't know about UNIX, I make up for with what I don't know about Linux and NT.

I joined this group for five reasons:

1) ego
2) chicks
3) ego
4) to learn more about UNIX
5) did I mention ego?

I am the world's greatest Chassidic dancer, I am probably great in bed – but I haven't been given any opportunities to perform - at least not with a partner — I am a drummer, and I play my organ. Women tell me I am a stud with a great body, but none of them want to marry me.

Is this group ready for me?"

The Idiot Who Can't Figure Out How to Unsubscribe

There is one on every mailing list. The person who has no idea how to unsubscribe from the list on their own. So, what do they do instead? They post an email to the group asking everyone how to do so. Here is an example of such an email:

"I'm going to be in Australia for a little while and won't be able to pick up my email. The last time I was out of the country, I couldn't get my email overseas and came back to the U.S. only to find about 5,000 messages in my email mailbox. Please note that I'm stupid and I forgot which email address I used to register with this server. It could be either one of the following two addresses:

joeloser@thisISP.net

OR

joeloser@thatISP.net

Here is how I answer them:

"I have a dozen things to say about that:

1 Do you recall how you subscribed to the list to begin with? Wasn't it by sending an email to majordomo? So, I bet if you sent another email to majordomo, instead of to the general list, then you wouldn't have to embarrass yourself in front of all of us by asking us to do it for you, especially since almost all of us don't have the power to do so anyways.

2   Since you posted this email from thisISP.net, I would bet a dollar to a doughnut that you registered to this list with your thisISP.net account.

3   Which account receives the posts from this group? Again, I would bet big bucks that it is your thisISP.net account. Now, what I would do is open an email that you receive from this group, hit the "reply" button, change the "To:" header to say majordomo@our_usergroup.org, and in the body of the email, write "unsubscribe our_usergroup", and take it from there.

4   When you fly to Australia, please remember to bring your airline tickets with you, and also be aware that the planes take off from LAX and NOT from downtown's Union Station.

5   Once you are onboard the jet, please pay special attention to the flight attendant's instructions on how to fasten your safety belt. This may prove to be especially tricky for you.

6   If you are really concerned that you may be un-subscribing from the wrong account, then maybe you should try un-subscribing from both accounts just to be safe.

7   Double check your itinerary to be sure they are sending you to Australia, and not Austria.

8   The instructions to unsubscribe are on our web site.

9   Our web site is www.our_usergroup.org.

10   You will need a browser to go to our web site.

11 If while on board the plane, you realize you should be going to Austria, please contact the nearest flight attendant immediately, and request that he or she hit you over the head with a sledge hammer.

12 Did I mention you need to send an email to majordomo?"

How to Deal With Idiots Who Can't Read

Every mailing list and user group has them – the idiots who can't follow directions. Here is how I deal with them:

"I noticed that my in-box today was filled up with all kinds of wonderful suggestions as to where to host our next meeting. And, yet, I see that the first post in this thread was sent from a list member who distinctly said "DO NOT POST YOUR SUGGESTIONS TO THE LIST....SEND YOUR SUGGESTIONS IN AN EMAIL DIRECTLY TO ME". Am I the only person who followed his instructions and sent to him a private email? English isn't my best language, and yet, I was able to understand what it is that he wrote. Can't anyone else in this group learn to read? Am I the only one who follows orders? Am I the only one who listens to their mom? Am I the only one who cleans up after himself?

I am tired of doing all of your housework for you. When are you going to get your lazy butt off of the couch and do something besides just sit around all day and play with your stupid computer? Can't you see I'm trying to get some work done for you? Why is this lousy house always so filthy? What if we have guests? Do you want them to think this is how we live? Do you want them to see me running around half-naked trying to clean up this pig's sty that you created because all you do all day is fiddle with your Hipware, or Slackware, or Slacks ware, or whatever the heck you call that crap which I have to compete with just to get some from you?

I haven't had it in months, but you wouldn't know it, because you are quite happy with your "uptime". When am I going to see some of that for myself?"

Answering a Question About Korn Shell

QUESTION: In ksh, how do I do a command replace
            ^this^tothat^ like I can in csh?

ANSWER: Simple. You can do this: ^ksh^csh^

I did this: ^rabbi_job^job_that_pays_real_money^

Right now, I am doing this:
^working^wasting_my_time_emailing_you^

And, I plan to do this:
^computers^career_in_comedy^

But, I wish I could do this:
^my_sports_car^wedding_ring^

But, I keep hearing this:

^I_wanna_get_married^what's_wrong_with_just_
being_friends?^

Which means all I am getting is this:

^normal_life^watching_HBO_re-runs_every_night"

The translation of that is this:

^serious_real_sex^HBO's_Real_Sex_series^

So, it could be that the only way I will get any after all, is with this:
^csh^ksh^

How to Offer Advice to Users

Say a user on the list asks a wide open question like:

"I have a list of SPARCstation NIC cards and their prices in front of me. Which one should I buy?"

How can anyone possibly answer that? Well, here is what I do –

"I can answer that for you, but first, to be able to offer the best advice, here is my 20 questions which I need addressed:

1) How much money are we looking to spend?

2) Do we want it new or used?

3) For which model Sparcstation?

4) How long do we want the warranty to last?

5) How long do we want the card to last?

6) How long do we want the Sparcstation to last?

7) How long do we want the Sopranos to last?

8) Should the Sopranos outlast the Sparcstation?

9) Should the Sparcstation outlast the card?

10) Should the card outlast the warranty?

11) Should the warranty outlast the shipping time?

12) For which model Sparcstation?

13) New or used?

14) How much money again?

15) Which UNIX group is this again?

16) How did I get here?

17) Where is my coffee?

18) Where are my pills?

19) What planet are we on?

20) What the heck is a NIC card?"

Chapter 7

Miscellaneous Geek Humor

2006 Edition of the Rabbs' Dictionary

Windows 2006   scheduled for release in early 2008, this is the most innovative creation promised to come from the wonderful folks at Redmond yet. This OS will be full of brand new concepts. Here are just a few promised: TCP/IP, BIND, RPC, NFS, automount, NIS, NIS+, Legato, a software RAID suite, X Windows, CDE, OpenWindows, a routing algorithm, csh, sh, ksh, and sendmail. It will also be fully compatible with all UNIX binaries, and fully support all GNU-ware.

Sun   the company which just filed a lawsuit in federal court to block the release of Windows 2006, claiming the OS is a total rip-off of its own Solaris 2.6.

Computers   what I did for a living way back when I was still an admin before I took over for Jay Leno on the Tonight Show.

Boulder Police   very close to finding the real killer of Jon Benet Ramsey. Prime suspect is now OJ Simpson.

Why Did the Chicken Cross the Road?

UNIX Chicken: Lays two dozen eggs, each grow up and individually make it across the road, only to argue with each other as to whom got there in the shortest time. All of the chicks report seeing the road kill remains of the NT chicken while crossing.

Sun/Solaris Chicken: Grows up in the gym pumping iron and wants to try crossing the road again, this time as a full-grown bulked-up chicken, and claims it can do it while carrying all of the other chickens on its back.

Oracle Chicken: Says to the SUN/Solaris chicken, "ok, carry me"

Netscape Chicken: Says it is looking for someone to carry it, too.

IBM Chicken: Says " I could've owned that road."

Linux Chicken: One of the fastest birds crossing the road due to the coaching it gets from thousands of its hippie supporters who come out to the road to cheer it on.

10 URLS I'd Like to See:

www.learn.how.to.drive.or.get.off.the.damn.road.com

www.capital.punishment.for.stopping.inside.the.crosswalk.org

www.give.me.a.radio.station.that.plays.music.in.the.morning.org

www.this.is.a.Constitutional.Republic.and.not.a.democracy.gov

www.quit.staring.at.me.unless.you.want.me.to.stare.back.net

www.no.overtime.work.from.me.until.the.government.stops.taking.all.of.the.extra.money.com

www.someone.tell.Maxine.Waters.to.sit.down.and.shut.up.gov

and, finally,

www.jokes.are.actors.if.they.don't.sing.and.dance.get.them.off.the.stage.org

which hyperlinks to:

www.your.jokes.suck.rabbi.so.take.me.off.from.your.frigin'.list.net

How is Fry's Like Disneyland?

You can never find a place to park.

It doesn't matter which month of the year, what day of the week, or what time of day you go, it is always packed.

Everyone working there knows less than you do about everything there.

Disneyland has 32 turnstiles and yet, there is still a huge line to pay to get in, while Fry's has 32 cashier windows, and yet, there is still a huge line to pay to get out.

Disneyland has many theme lands, while Fry's has many disorganized departments.

Disneyland	you go to Tomorrowland to check out late night disco
Fry's	you go to the stereo speakers area to check out Rabbs' all day dancing
Disneyland	you stop to watch the Electric Light Parade
Fry's	you stop to watch four different ball games on four different big screens
Disneyland	you wait an hour for a ride
Fry's	you wait an hour for a salesperson to arrive
Disneyland	never captures the memory it seems you want to restore
Fry's	never has the memory SIMMs you want to replace

| Disneyland | refinished park |
| Fry's | refurbished parts |

| Disneyland | can never find a phone when you need one |
| Fry's | can never find a VTech 9000 when it is on sale |

| Disneyland | you are told those attractions and that part of the park aren't open this time of year |
| Fry's | you are told these appliances with those advertised prices aren't available in this store location |

| Disneyland | you can't wait for summer hours to check out the rides at night |
| Fry's | you can't wait for Friday's L.A. Times to arrive to check out the four-page ad |

| Disneyland | for an hour in line you must listen to some yutz tell his wife how great it is to get away from his office |
| Fry's | for an hour in line you must listen to some putz tell his wife how great it is to upgrade his M$ Office |

and finally,

| Disneyland | everyone leaves wearing mouse ears or some dumb novelty item |
| Fry's | everyone leaves carrying 50 floppies for 99 cents after rebate |

See Bill Run...

See Bill.

See Bill run.

See Bill annoy a huge part of this country.

See Bill lie, cheat, deny, and steal.

See Bill obstruct justice and abuse his power.

See Bill get caught.

See Bill get caught with his pants down.

See Bill get taken to court.

See Bill become Janet Reno's target.

See Bill lie under oath in both a civil deposition and in a federal court.

See Bill create negative spin about his persecutors.

See Bill lie to his closest friends and counsel.

See Bill lie to Congress.

See Bill lie to the American public.

See Bill up to his eyeballs in civil and criminal legal bills.

See Bill have to force Congress to take action despite the fact that doing so isn't popular in this country.

See Bill able to remain one of the most popular and powerful men in the world despite all of his negative attention.

See Bill continue to attack and try to destroy his enemies abroad while Congress and the courts are attacking him in Washington DC and even outside of the beltway.

See Bill take advantage of the fact Americans don't understand the issues.

See Bill prove "the masses are asses".

See Bill get away with anything.

See Bill tie up our government.

See Bill bring this country to its knees.

See Bill refuse to resign.

See Bill try to extend his trial as long as possible in an attempt to postpone the inevitable.

See Bill force delays in the investigation and trials.

See Bill blame delays on his opponents.

See Bill remain the leader of the strongest empire the world has ever known.

And, finally, boys and girls,

See Bill delay the verdict long enough to release his Windows 2000.

That jotd was much funnier when Clinton was still president and Windows 2000 had still yet to be released.

The Top 10 UNIX Geek Pick-Up Lines

10   Let me help you out of your shell.

9   Let's be like two packets and collide.

8   Let's do it on the desktop.

7   I'd love to make it with you (but who will do the pushing?).

6   You look like you need a good listener.

5   I write in C, so I know how to use my pointer

4   Hey, you've got nice mount points

3   Let me slide my pipe in between your commands.

2   I have experience with the hard mount.

and the number 1 pick-up line:

1   Hey baby, UNIX admins do it with greater uptime.

Chapter 8

All About My JOTD List

The UnixRabbi's JOTD is "Must Read CC:"

Look at what the critics are saying:

Bill Gates: "It is more scaleable than Solaris"

James Gosling: "Read once, laugh everywhere"

Steve Jobs: "The best part of jotd is that Microsoft doesn't own it"

Linus Torvalds: "I support jotd as long as it remains free"

Scott McNealy: "It meets our standards to be considered
                        100% Pure Ha Ha"

Marc Andreessen: "Jotd has the market share, so I am sure unixrabbi is
                        the way of the future. Did I mention I developed the
                        first jotd?"

Al Gore: "Jotd is funny, and environmentally friendly. I used to
                        read them while in the White House when I was put on
                        hold while making fundraising calls to Asia.
                        Did I mention I invented the first jotd?"

Larry Ellison: "Finally someone is using the idea of one jotd server
                        and many networked clients"

Bob Metcalfe: "That unixrabbi has one twisted pair of personalities"

Steve Ballmer: "It is my honor to announce our latest
innovation – M$jotd"

Dennis Rodman: "I get so drunk with laughter that I want to take
unixrabbi to Las Vegas and marry him"

unixrabbi's parents: "Vous lachs du?"

Bob Lewis
(InfoWorld columnist):   "Management Speak: 'We can't have those jotds in
our workplace'
Translation: 'As soon as you leave my office, I am
getting back to reading them' "

Bill Clinton: "I did not have sexual relations with any woman on
the jotd list. I never asked anyone to sign up. Depends
on how you define jotd"

Hillary Clinton: "Jotd is something to chuckle through while waiting
to give a deposition"

Linda Tripp: "If jotd was audible, I'd tape 22 hours of it"

Bob Dole: "Bob Dole says jotd works better than
Viagra"

Ross Perot: "Folks, that giant sucking sound you'll hear will be
from thousands of folks being drawn to jotd"

Dan Quayle: "How do you spell jotd?"

Barbara Boxer:	"Blah, blah, blah, jotd is really funny. Blah, blah, blah, jotd is not funny at all (how am I doing in the latest polls?)"
O.J. Simpson:	"Funniest thing since I said I was searching after the real killers"

and finally,

Monica Lewinsky:	"Jotd blows"

And now, JOTD, "Must Read CC:" pauses for a Word from Our Sponsor —

a Snickers bar from the machine	65 cents
3 cans of Mountain Dew	$1.95
1 pack of Marlboro Lights	$2.25
1 Cohiba Cuban cigar you were saving	$20
2 bottles of Heineken from the fridge	$2.50
1 joint of Kona Gold that no one wanted to share	$11
2 cups of flavored coffee	$3
2 lines of coke	$10
1 speed tablet	$5

2 thick crust pizzas delivered, plus tip $20

staying up all night and hacking
into the payroll database   priceless

If a credit card could handle all of that, I'd order one. :)

More JOTD Reviews

Chelsea Clinton   "My mother says the opponents of jotd are just part of a vast right wing conspiracy."

Ralph Nader   "Don't blame JOTD on me."

Howard Stern   "Robin, jotd is the King of All Email...that's right...Baba Booey...but I'm still kicking its ass in 5 cities...it will eventually be my little doggie...He refers to himself in third person as "the unixrabbi". What pretentious crap. I don't get it. It's almost like he's become a fictional character. What's that all about? This guy is so full of himself. Well, pal, you're not fooling anyone. You're still my little doggy and you will bow down to me. Bark, doggy. Fred, play the barking noises...And, what the hell is Unix anyways? Robin, have you ever heard of Unix?...I didn't think so...And, what kind of rabbi writes those kind of jokes?...He should be ashamed of himself...He is a disgrace... kush mir un tuchas, rabbi...kiss my lily white ass...And, Jackie, aren't we learning way too much about this guy's personal life?...Robin, this is why I have to get out of this business. Look at what I'm competing with. I can't take it anymore. I'm telling you, I'm going to finish my contract

and then, I'm out of here. That's right…I
can't do this anymore. This time I mean it,
Robin…And all of you can just gae kochen
al ha yam…He's just jealous of me…did I
mention I wrote two best selling books,
made the best motion picture of our
lifetime…clap,clap…thank you, Robin…"

The Top 10 responses I received from my JOTD list members after I announced I was considering a career in comedy because some-one told me they heard Dr. Laura Schlessinger read one of my JOTD's on the air:

10   "well, if it doesn't work out, you could always be her personal comic"

9   "maybe she can post your jokes next to her naked photos on the web"

8   "as if this country doesn't have enough Jewish comics"

7   "30,000 unemployed comedians in this country, and you want to be another one of them?"

6   "if your boss catches you writing jokes all day, comedy may be the only career left for you"

5   "Rabbs, if you are serious about a career change, then you *are* a comedian"

4   "have you been smoking something again?"

3   "just tell me when you make the move so that I can sell off my Microsoft stocks"

2 "don't quit your day job"

and the no. 1 response to my announcement was:

1 "someone admitted to listening to Dr. Laura?"

Chapter 9

Signing Off

The UnixRabbi's Famous Tag Lines

All of my jotds, which I ever emailed, finished with a signature line. I thought it would be appropriate to conclude this book by sharing some of my favorites:

— the unixrabbi
There are a lot of Jewboys in the computer field, but there is only one unixrabbi.

— the unixrabbi
May the All-Mighty grant you the wisdom to know the difference between right and wrong, good and evil, SUN and Microsoft.

— the unixrabbi
I have worked at three companies in the past year and I am still sitting in the same room.

— the unixrabbi
Proving there is the Right way, the Wrong way, and the Remer way

— the unixrabbi
TECHNO-CLERGY GEEK WITH ATTITUDE

— the unixrabbi
Ah sheinum dunck fer lessen meine unterschrift.

— the unixrabbi

UNIX — not just an OS, but the geek form of birth control

— the unixrabbi

UNIX, because a computer is a terrible thing to waste.

— the unixrabbi

A day without email from Rabbs is like a day without sex.

— the unixrabbi

It is all about me. Me, me, me. I love me.
I love to read what I write on the Internet.
I love to stare at myself in the mirrors.
I love the attention I get. I love the laughter you receive.
But, most of all, I love me.

— the unixrabbi

You are either on my team or you don't exist.

— the unixrabbi

Do not incur the wrath of the Rabbs.

— the unixrabbi

Y2K disasters turned out to be nothing that a few hundred billion dollars couldn't prevent.

— the unixrabbi

It is not how much you know, but how much money you make pretending to know.

— the unixrabbi

Better to be an overpaid idiot than an underpaid guru.

— the unixrabbi

Visit http://www.rabbs.com — not just another dot comedy, but a pre-IPO start-up where funny bones are tickled daily!

— the unixrabbi

Expertise in: Chassidic dancing and UNIX, but the following is everything I know about women:

Chapter 10

About the Author

Who Am I?

Finally, you ask "Who are you?"

Fair question.

I am a UNIX network administrator with eight years of professional experience, and I am a Sun Certified Solaris Administrator and a Sun Certified Network Administrator.

In addition, I am America's Favorite Rabbi Comic, performing groundbreaking stand-up comedy regularly at the hottest nightclubs in Southern California, including the World Famous Comedy Store in Hollywood, and the World Famous Improv in Irvine and in Ontario, CA, where I am seen below in an action shot:

Would You Let That Man Touch Your UNIX System?

Yes, I am a Chasidic rabbi and I used to work full-time in that capacity before entering the naturally combining worlds of computers and comedy.

CPSIA information can be obtained at www.ICGtesting.com
Printed in the USA
BVOW05s1915051215

429438BV00001BA/40/P